# Wings t.

by
Stevina Southwell

Wings to Fly

First published in the United Kingdom in 2017
by
Stevina Southwell

Scripture quotations [marked NIV] taken from the Holy Bible, New International Version Anglicised Copyright © 1979, 1984, 2011 Biblica. Used by permission of Hodder & Stoughton Ltd, an Hachette UK company

'NIV' is a registered trademark of Biblica UK, trademark number 1448790.

Quote on Page 3 used by permission of Jeff A Benner from the Ancient Hebrew Research Centre.

Cover design & illustration by Helen Clifford.

ISBN: 978-1544659473

# The Bible and Poetry

"Approximately 75% of the Old Testament is poetry. All of Psalms and Proverbs are Hebrew poetry. Even the book of Genesis is full Poetry.

There are several reasons the Hebrews used poetry, much of the Torah was sung and was easier to sing too, poetry and songs are easier to memorize than straight texts, Parallel poetry (as in Genesis 1) emphasizes something of great importance, as the creation story is.

The rabbis believed that if something is worth saying, it is worth saying beautifully."

Jeff A Benner

# Acknowledgements

I am thankful that God has given me a gift to write in rhyme. He has been with me every step of the way.

To my dear Grandfather Harry, a true man of faith. No matter what life threw at him, he always had God's smile on his face.

I also thank God for my beloved Grandmother Emerald, who believed in the power of persistent prayers and never giving up.

To all of you who have ever prayed and encouraged me on this journey may God richly bless you!

To my dear husband Jamie, for his love, constant help and input into my writing.

Additional thanks to:
Pastor Andrew White and Family; Helen Clifford; Paul and Shelia Fronda; Margaret Hague; The Lupikisha Family; Liz Weedon, Kev Crookes, Dariusz Chorzepa, Nikki Holbrook and Roke Writers.

A special thanks for you, the reader.  My prayer for you is that God will richly bless you. As you read, may the words touch your heart; I hope you find laughter and comfort.

No matter what you are going through, remember God has promised he will never leave you or forsake you.

'No one will be able to stand against you all the days of your life. As I was with Moses, so I will be with you; I will never leave you nor forsake you.'
Joshua 1:5 [NIV]

# Contents

The Bible and Poetry ............................................................ iii

Acknowledgements ............................................................. iv

Contents ........................................................................... v

Transformation & Life's Journey ......................................... 9

    Butterfly ..................................................................... 10

    The Flower ................................................................. 11

    Flourish ...................................................................... 13

    The Raging Butterfly .................................................. 14

Love ............................................................................... 15

    Jesus Lover of My Soul ............................................... 16

    Love .......................................................................... 17

    God's Love Poem ....................................................... 18

    Will You Miss Me ........................................................ 19

People ............................................................................ 21

    Pastors ...................................................................... 22

    Mother ....................................................................... 23

    My Friend ................................................................... 24

    Sister ......................................................................... 25

    God's People .............................................................. 26

    Daughter of Zion ......................................................... 27

    The Gift ...................................................................... 28

    Angel ......................................................................... 29

## Hope in Despair .................................................. 31

In The Arms of Jesus ............................................ 32

Losing ....................................................................... 33

Pray Until Something Happens (PUSH) ............... 34

Joy Comes In the Morning .................................... 35

Pit of Despair ......................................................... 36

Silence ...................................................................... 37

Dark Cloud of Emotion ......................................... 38

Rejoice ...................................................................... 39

Rise Up ..................................................................... 40

Stronger .................................................................... 41

Midnight Hour ......................................................... 42

## Bible Events ...................................................... 45

Jonah and the Whale ............................................. 46

The Packed Lunch ................................................... 48

Donkey ...................................................................... 50

The Letter ................................................................ 53

## Seasons and Events .......................................... 57

New Year .................................................................. 58

Spring ........................................................................ 59

Seasons ..................................................................... 60

What Does Christmas Mean? ................................ 61

Birthday .................................................................... 62

## Life ....................................................... 63

Grace .................................................... 64

The I Poem ............................................ 65

Israel ................................................... 66

Health .................................................. 67

Keep Calm and Carry On ........................ 68

Israel part 2 ......................................... 69

## Poems of Faith ...................................... 71

Holy Spirit ............................................ 72

Wind .................................................... 73

Mirror .................................................. 74

Your Face ............................................. 75

Seven ................................................... 76

## Gift Poems ............................................ 77

Bag of Gold ........................................... 78

The Blessing .......................................... 80

Salvation Prayer .................................... 81

## About The Author ................................. 82

## Poetry Therapy .................................... 83

# Transformation & Life's Journey

# Butterfly

The butterfly symbolises freedom,
and something being reborn.
When we lose someone we love;
We feel our hearts are torn.

A butterfly has no cares or fears;
there's no sadness, there's no tears.

Its wings as it flutters, send out its love;
It's looking down as it flies above.

You play amongst the flowers, and rest in the trees.
God made you so beautiful, peaceful and at ease.

You're going towards heaven and there you will find your rest;
Because you are a butterfly, God made you the very best.

When the caterpillar is transformed into a butterfly it becomes a new
creation. When we become born again we are a new creation in Christ and
we have freedom from sin through him.

'Therefore, if anyone is in Christ, the new creation has come: The old has
gone, the new is here!'
2 Corinthians 5:17 [NIV]

# The Flower

I am the flower of beauty and power;
I am a flower.

I was there from the beginning when you entered the earth;
I was the sweet-peas given to your mother, to celebrate your birth.

As a child when the summers were hot and hazy;
I was the flower you picked, the pretty small daisy.

As you blossomed and went out on your first date;
I was the dozen red roses that were left by the gate.

I was the carnations, lavender, tulips and jasmine, a wonderful
bouquet;
I was with you, on your grand wedding day.

All through your life I have been there for you;
Birthdays, anniversaries and Christmas too!

Through the good and bad times and when you were ill;
I was the friend that was silent and still.

The days, the months, the years, have passed;
And so to eternity, you go at last.

For I'm now the Lily, that's part of the grief;
I am the poppy on your funeral wreath.

For you my petals like arms outstretched, I'll wait:
When you pass through heaven's glorious gate;

I have been with you every single hour;
As God is the flower of beauty and power.

God is with us during all of life's stages. From birth to death God is with us.

# Flourish

You are born to flourish;
and rise on eagles' wings.

You are born to flourish;
Do exploits and great things.

You will flourish like the palm tree; there's fruit for you to bear;
You will grow like the cedar in Lebanon and nothing can compare.

You will flourish in the courts of God, his praises you will sing;
You are born to flourish; and you are born to win.

Based on: Palms 92 [NIV]

# The Raging Butterfly

Outside I am beautiful, with colourful fragile wings;
Yet inside I feel the pain, that my caterpillar self brings.
No one understands me; I feel they do not try;
I have to conform to their ways; I feel I'm living a lie.

I feel a rage within me, I want to shout and scream;
Still they do not listen and I'm not seen.
I try to explain my feelings, to convey my one true self;
If only they would listen, my words would give them wealth.

I feel a rage within me, I want to scream and shout;
I feel my lips moving but nothing's coming out.

I know I have a calling, which the creator has planned;
Am I ready to spread my wings and ready to take a stand?

I am the raging butterfly; I do have something to say;
No longer am I a caterpillar, I have wings and can fly away;

To someone who will listen and see the real me;
I will spread my big strong wings, and truly I'll be free.

There are times in life when people don't see our potential; we may feel
ignored and not good enough. God says he has good plans for you.

'For I know the plans I have for you,' declares the Lord, "plans to prosper
you and not to harm you, plans to give you hope and a future.'
Jeremiah 29:11 [NIV]

# Love

# Jesus Lover of My Soul

Jesus, lover of my soul;
Mend me, father, make me whole.

Help me to walk in all your ways;
Fill my mouth with laughter and praise.

Give me strength to face each day;
Protect and watch me as I pray.

Help me, Lord, to do your will;
Let me hear your voice that's gentle and still.

Thank you, Father, for sending your Son from above;
Thank you for your grace, mercy and love.

Jesus, lover of my soul,
Thank you for making me complete and whole.

# Love

Love is patient; love is kind and keeps no records of wrong;
It keeps us going when we can stand no more, but keeps our faith strong.

Love can leave you broken and love can make you feel good;
Love can be confusing and sometimes misunderstood.

Love is not about the hearts and flowers or a love song that you hear;
It's about compassion, helping others and wiping another's tear.

Being able to give forgiveness demonstrates true love;
Remember the Father has forgiven you by his grace and mercy from above.

When you love someone you put their needs above your own;
And then this love comes back to you and you never feel alone.

The greatest commandment is to love your neighbour more than yourself;
By doing this you get an inheritance of abundant wealth.

The greatest love of all is when one can lay down his life for his friends;
That is what true love is, a love that never ends.

# God's Love Poem

Love is patient; Love is Kind;
Love is true when hearts are aligned.

Love keeps no records of when we are wrong;
Love encourages and keeps each other strong.

Love is not boastful or filled with pride;
Love is the hand that is willing to guide.

Love enriches and does not smother;
Love does not put itself above another;

Love is not self-seeking;
It uses gentle words when speaking.

Love is self-sacrifice that never wavers or swings;
Love gives hope, endurance and bears all things.

Love is the reason that we all live;
Love is the greatest gift that we can give.

Based on 1 Corinthians 13:4-7

# Will You Miss Me

Will you miss me when I'm gone, my face you'll see no more;
Will you shed a tear for me or just walk out the door?

Will you always be bitter and not have forgiveness in your heart?
Will you always choose anger to rip your soul apart?

You were kind and loving with goodness in your eyes;
All I see is hatred now and you I do despise.

Broken hearts can be mended; they just need love and time.
Don't make love a bad thing, don't make it into a crime.

The Bible says we should bind our hearts with cords that cannot be
broken.
Remember God sent his son through love, the ultimate love token.

Love is kind, patient and keeps no records of wrongs;
Go back to the one you love, that's where your heart belongs.

# People

# Pastors

Please pray for your Pastor, they serve you from the heart;
Please pray for your Pastor that they remain strong and able to do
their part.

Pray that Jesus lifts them and gives knowledge and wisdom too;
Don't just wait expecting what your Pastor can do for you.

We must pray for our Shepherd, for God's mighty grace;
It's hard being a Pastor, many challenges they face.

If we want to grow as people, we must first sow a seed;
If we want to grow as people, we must pray for those who lead.

Make their burdens easy make their yokes be light;
It doesn't matter when you pray for them, in the day or night.

If you want to get good teaching, you really can't go wrong;
Keep praying for your Pastor and they will get really strong.

Pray that God will bless them and that church will grow;
Jesus will do the rest and let his blessings overflow.

As you watch over your flock, Jesus will watch over you.
Please pray for your Pastors, it's God's instruction and your biblical
duty too.

Thank you Pastors around the world for all the work you do
There is a blessing waiting in heaven and a crown of glory for you.

# Mother

Mothers of the world, we honour you today;
May your lives be filled with God's favour, this is what we pray.

May God give you wisdom to keep your household strong.
May he give you good health so you may live long.

May you feel the love of Jesus resting in your heart;
May his blessings be upon you, never to depart.

May the work of your hands be bountiful and never be in lack.
May he shine a lamp upon your feet, to keep you on the right
track.

I pray he gives you patience in everything you do.
Remember you're a blessing and very precious too.

M is for God's Mercy that he has shown to you;
O is for Obedience that will see you through.
T is for your Tenderness and your loving care;
H is for your Heart, so willing to share;
E is for Eternal, your never-ending love;
R is for Redemption given from the Lord above.

You are very special, there will be no other;
that's why I'm so thankful that I can call you Mother.

'As a mother comforts her child, so will I comfort you; and you will be
comforted over Jerusalem.'
Isaiah 66:13 [NIV]

# My Friend

To have a friend like you is a blessing and divine;
You are always there for me; you listen and take the time.

You are there in the good times and also in the bad;
You comfort me when I'm lonely and when I'm feeling sad.

You never judge or condemn me when I do things wrong;
And when I'm at my weakest you make feel very strong.

Friendships are important, they are ever true;
One day I hope I will be as good a Friend as you.

# Sister

Having a sister in Christ like you;
Is sweeter than the morning dew.

Your love for others is plain to see;
You are a true sister to me.

I thank you for your kindness and your love;
You are like an angel sent from above.

Thank you for your wisdom and care;
Thank you for upholding me in prayer.

May God richly bless you for all your love and grace;
May he give you peace and keep the smile upon your face.

# God's People

There is no time to slumber, no time to sleep;
Jesus has asked, "Will you feed my sheep?"

The sick need healing for all of their suffering and pain;
The broken need comfort so their souls can rejoice again.

Our God is a God of miracles, his wonders to perform;
He's a God of mercy and will get us through the storm.

The words of the Lord are steadfast; the words of the Lord are
true;
Like silver purified in the furnace, that's his portion for you.

We must pray for one another and keep each other strong;
We must learn to forgive each other when we are wrong.

We were made by our creator from the heavens above;
We were made in his image and we must reflect his love.

No matter what the devil has stolen, and all the lies he's told;
God has promised us restoration, which is seven-fold.

There is nothing impossible that Jesus cannot do.
He is the resurrected King and wants his best for you.

# Daughter of Zion

Do not cry my daughter God has seen your heart;
He has seen the work of your hands, which sets you apart.

You have laboured in God's vineyard and you will receive your
reward;
God's bounty will overtake you, his treasures for you he's stored.

Remember you are a daughter of Zion, God's very own;
One day you will be seated with him in heaven and sitting by his
throne.

Jesus has seen your heart and will guide you through;
Don't worry if others mistreat or have done wrong by you.

Jesus lives within you and you are bold as the lion.
Remember you are his child, beautiful daughter of Zion.

# The Gift

A child is so precious, what a glorious gift;
A little soul so gentle, our hearts rejoice and lift.

They are placed into our lives to give them love and care;
We commit them to our Lord and saviour in our daily prayer.

Jesus was born as a baby too;
So he could do something wonderful for you.

The Father sent his beautiful Son from a manger to the cross;
What a wonderful gift for all mankind so we didn't suffer loss.

I thank you God for your precious child, so wonderful and new.
I pray that God's hand will be on your life and always follow you.

Remember that you are a gift so precious in God's sight;
My prayer is that you'll put him in your heart and love him with
all your might.

'Every good and perfect gift is from above, coming down from the Father
of the heavenly lights, who does not change like shifting shadows.'
James 1:17 [NIV]

# Angel

Don't worry, my pretty, God is smiling on you;
Don't worry, my precious child, he will see you through.

He will send an angel from heaven, who will protect you every day;
He will hold your hand and guide you every step of the way.

Never be discouraged, know that you are not alone;
God has given you an angel of your very own.

# Hope in Despair

# In The Arms of Jesus

In the arms of Jesus that's where I will be tonight;
No more suffering or pain, what a pure delight.

Jesus will wipe the tears of the loved ones I've left behind.
He will give them joy and peace of mind;

Now I'm in the arms of Jesus, my soul is now at rest.
I have my Lord's salvation and I am truly blessed.

'When you lie down, you will not be afraid; when you lie down, your sleep
will be sweet.'
Proverbs 3:24 [NIV]

# Losing

Losing the ones we love so much is too hard to bear;
Our hearts are sad and broken and it makes us shed a tear.

As long as we have good memories they will help you through;
Your loved one will always be in your heart and everything you do.

When you see a flower it will make you smile;
Your sadness and sorrow will only last a while.

Focus on the happy times and things that made you laugh;
Your loved one will be close to you and walking in your path.

# Pray Until Something Happens (PUSH)

Jesus loves his children; he loves to hear us pray;
He loves to see us sing, dance and worship him in every way.

Please do not get discouraged when things seem to go awry;
The Lord is doing something special for you just continue to pray.

God wants you to be the head and certainly not the tail;
He is always true to his word, which will never fail.

Trust in the Lord with all your heart and he will see you through.
Just pray to the Lord Jesus, as his word is ever true.

Pray for God's forgiveness, let your heart be pure;
When you are cleansed and holy, your blessings will be sure.

I thank you, Lord for listening; I know that I'll PUSH through;
Pray until something happens and God will do it for you.

# Joy Comes In the Morning

Joy comes in the morning, when darkness is out of sight;
God is going to bless you with all of his heavenly might.

Your mourning will turn to dancing as you lift your hands in praise;
Declaring the glory of Jesus all the rest of your days.

God has heard your crying, his heart aches for you;
when you feel forgotten he'll do something new.

Do not get discouraged he will bring you through;
Jesus really loves you and wants his best for you.

'For his anger lasts only a moment, but his favour lasts a lifetime; weeping
may stay for the night, but rejoicing comes in the morning.'
Psalm 30:5 [NIV]

# Pit of Despair

Oh Lord, do you hear my prayer;
As I am in the pit of despair.

I cry to you all night long;
My joy, my peace, seems to have gone.

How long, Oh Lord, will I have to wait?
For you to answer and determine my fate.

Lord, are you really by my side?
Why does it feel your face you hide?

Lord, bring me out from this pit of despair;
Father, hear my heavenly prayer.

'I call on the LORD in my distress, and he answers me.'
Psalm 120:1 [NIV]

# Silence

I listened out for you today;
As I read your book and started to pray.

I really wanted to hear your voice;
So I could sing and rejoice.

But there was silence, I could not hear;
Had you gone was my fear?

Was there something I'd done wrong?
Or should I sing a different song?

Lord, I need to hear from you today;
Please talk with me while I pray.

I need to know that you are near;
Please take away my doubt and fear.

Father, Father, please bring laughter and joy to me;
And let me hear your voice so I can be free.

# Dark Cloud of Emotion

Oh dark cloud of emotion, I wish you would leave me alone;
You chain me up and fill my cup with sadness that makes me
groan.

I really want to be free of you and let the sunshine fill my life;
I want to have a song in my heart, live in blessing and not in strife.

How I long for the touch of God to mould me with his hands;
I long for a life full of joy and looking forward to all God's plans.

I want the darkness to melt away and be washed by your precious
blood;
I want to feel God's love and true salvation engulf me like a flood.

How I long for my heavy heart to sing and dance before the Lord;
How I long for my own testimony from Jesus and in him is my
reward.

I want the love of Jesus to be steadfast in my heart;
No more clouds of emotion, a brand new day, a brand new start.

# Rejoice

When God answered my prayer I declared with a shout;
Sing 'Hallelujah' and let my joy come out!

How could I have doubted you would do it for me?
Thank you, Father for this is your day, we celebrate the victory.

I bow down, worship you and praise your holy name;
You are worthy to be praised and on the throne you reign.

You took me from the pit and set me on high;
My tears have turned to laughter, no more do I cry.

I sing and dance before you as you are my Lord;
You have been with me through those long nights I've endured.

Thank you, thank you, Jesus you have done so much;
You have turned it round for me in a single touch.

What seemed so impossible was nothing to you;
How great is my Jesus, there is nothing you cannot do.

Lord, I want to praise you, you've shown me your grace;
You are so wonderful, I see your glorious face.

Restoration and recovery seven-fold have been given;
I know my Jesus is Lord and he has truly risen.

Sorry when I doubted and I nearly gave up;
Thank you for standing with me and filling up my cup.

# Rise Up

Rise up, rise up, you people;
God has heard your cry.
Just trust in the Lord Jesus and you will live and never die.

Jesus wants to lift you up and give you a garment of praise;
Beauty for your ashes throughout the coming days.

Take the oil of gladness and put a smile upon my face;
I will live in Zion, my heavenly dwelling place.

Although my heart may be heavy and I may feel all alone;
My God will not forsake me as he is still on the throne.

You are more than a conqueror, your affliction won't last long;
Rise up, rise up, you people for Victory is your song.

# Stronger

You are stronger than you think;
You have been through many trials that bought you to the brink.

You have inner qualities that you may not even know;
Yet through your love and kindness they really start to show.

I wish you every happiness and success in all you do.
I pray for peace and comfort and that all your dreams come true.

# Midnight Hour

Lift your voice to Jesus, let him hear your praise;
Let him hear your singing, let your voices raise.

Let your singing break the stronghold;
Don't let the devil take your soul.
Make it your mission, make praise your goal.

Praise him in the good times;
Praise him when things are bad.
Praise him in your darkest hour and when you're feeling sad.

Jesus will up lift you and take you through the storm;
He'll take you through the midnight hour, to the breaking of your dawn.

Don't let the devil defeat you;
You are programmed to win.
Jesus came and saved you and delivered you from sin.

Jesus will take you through the storm and through the midnight hour;
You have the victory and Jesus' mighty power.

God will fight your battle and knock your Goliath down;
He'll save you from the Egyptians and he won't let you drown.

You are God's beloved and he will see you through;
Look unto Jesus, he will do it for you.

Praise him in the morning; praise him in the night;
Keep close to Jesus and you WILL WIN the fight.

Jesus will uplift you and take you through the storm;
He'll take you through the midnight hour, to the breaking of your dawn.

# Bible Events

# Jonah and the Whale

I'm going to tell of a tale of Jonah and the whale:
You see God told Jonah to go to Nineveh but Jonah tried to derail.

Jonah thought he was clever and God would never know.
So he got on a boat and planned a very different course to go.

Jonah thought he'd got away from what the Lord had planned;
So God had to take matters up in his own mighty hand.

A storm did rage the waters high as it buffeted the boat;
Umm, oh Jonah, I bet you've got no time to gloat.

Overboard went cargo and all the people's stuff;
This did not abate the storm, it still was getting rough.

Oh poor Jonah, what's the right thing to do?
The next thing that should go overboard really should be you.

So Jonah was thrown into the sea and swallowed by a whale;
But this is not the end of Jonah's fishy tail.

Three days and nights he lingered inside the giant whale;

Bet you wished you'd gone to Nineveh now, instead of provoking the gale.
The whale spat him out, on Nineveh's sandy shore;
And off he went to the people, to preach as instructed before.

You see when God wants you to do something you can try to run and hide.
But Jesus will find you and remove your foolish pride.

When God has a purpose for you, know it can never fail.
Just remember Jonah and his time stuck inside the whale.

'Now the LORD provided a huge fish to swallow Jonah, and Jonah was in the belly of the fish three days and three nights.'
Jonah 1:17 [NIV]

Read the book of Jonah and see how God extends his Grace and Mercy even when we disobey him.

# The Packed Lunch

"Will you pack some lunch for me?" the young boy asked his
mother;
"I'm going to see the teacher; they say he's not like any other."

"Okay," she said, "I will see what I can make."
So she set to work and five loaves she did bake.

She looked in her pantry and spotted a small round dish.
When she looked inside, she found two small fish.

She wrapped the food and blessed it and gave it to her son.
"You go and run along now, I hope you do have fun!"
The young boy thanked his mother for all that she had done.

The boy was just so happy, with anticipation in his heart;
Everyone was talking about this teacher, what set him apart?

As he reached the end of the valley the crowd was just so large;
He weaved his way through the people but didn't push or barge.

Then the crowd was silent as the teacher started to speak;
They listened so intently not a word they would critique.

Hours and hours went by but no one fell asleep;
The teacher noticed they were hungry and needed food to eat.

The young boy gave his lunch to a disciple who was nearby.
"Give it to the teacher!" he said with a cheerful cry.

The bread and fish were given and the teacher blessed the food;
Then what happens next is so complex to conclude.

The five loaves and the fish were given to 5,000 to be precise;
No-one was left feeling hungry and the food was very nice.

At the end of the meal there were leftover baskets, so I'm told;
The young boy couldn't believe the miracle that did unfold.

The boy went and told his mother about his lunch and what he'd seen;
There was no fast food restaurant, cafe or canteen.

God can take the simple things and make them into much.
All it needs is faith, his word and his gentle touch.

Based on Luke 9:10-17

# Donkey

No one really notices me;
I'm just a humble donkey,

I travel and carry heavy loads;
Along the dusty and uneven roads.

I remember once when I was young;
I went on a journey that was so long.

I carried a young girl, a mother to be;
I think her name was something like Mary.

We walked for miles and sometimes days;
Along the paths and country ways.

Then we arrived at David's City;
Nowhere to stay, which was a pity.

The hustle and bustle of Bethlehem;
I did not know what would happen then.

Innkeepers had no room at their places;
I could see the despair on Mary and Joseph's faces.

We then made our way to a cattle shed;
Where Mary made her baby's bed.

I heard a cry in the night and then I saw a flash of light;
In the morning I saw Mary holding her precious baby tight.

Shepherds came from the hills and worshipped on their knees
Who is this child they are so willing to please?

Wise men came from afar;
It was told they were guided by a bright shining star.

Gifts for the child of Frankincense, Gold and Myrrh;
In my heart I could feel a stir.

I don't understand these things; of the infant and what his
presence brings.
I think he must be someone special, someone full of love;
I think I also saw angels singing from above.

I will not forget that glorious night; all those things, what a
wondrous sight.
I saw the child looking with love at me;
Yes, me a humble small donkey.

Then many years later I saw those same eyes smiling back at me;
You see the man child now was the age of 33.

He took my colt and rode him through Jerusalem's town;
One minute the people were singing, then next they tore him
down.

They beat him; spat at him, my beautiful baby boy.
He is the light of the world, who gives us hope and joy.

I was told he was crucified and died for all we've done wrong;
And he is Father God's one and only son.

The Good News is he rose again, and is very much alive;
If this wasn't so, you humans would not be able to survive.

The cross, you see he died on can be found upon my back.
Yes, that's what Jesus gave us donkeys and it is a fact.

I may seem insignificant but I played a part;
I know that Jesus loves me and I am in his heart.

# The Letter

I wrote a letter to Jesus to say sorry for my sin;
I didn't know how to start it, or even where to begin.

I thanked you for the gift of Christmas and for being born;
I didn't know what suffering you would endure, or the bitter scorn.

You rode upon a donkey through the cobbled street;
The people sang "Hosanna!" and laid palm leaves at your feet.

They shouted, "Glory! This is the Messiah, Saviour and our King!"
They didn't know that you were sent, to save them from their sin.

You went into the garden with your friends to watch and pray;
The one who kissed you on the cheek, was the one who would betray.

Your friends could not even stay awake, as you sweated drops of blood;
How your heart ached with sorrow and engulfed you like a flood.

The one you loved denied you, three times in a row;
He was asked if he knew you, but Peter just said "No!"

Betrayed, denied and wounded by the ones you love;
Yet you forgave them with your mercy from above.

They whipped your back for good measure;
Hoped the people would be satisfied;
But the same ones who cried "Hosanna!" now said "Crucify!"

Your back was ripped and broken and torn to the bone;
By your stripes we are healed, we don't complain or moan.

The Roman, Pontius Pilate, did not know what to do;
So he took a bowl of water and washed his hands of you.

You were accused falsely, of things you had not done;
The blameless one called Jesus, the Father's only son.

They spat at you and tore your beard and mocked you to your face;
You suffered all this for us, to prepare a heavenly place.

You were handed to the people, who placed a thorn crown on your head;
The mob was very angry and wished that you were dead.

And yet you did not say a word, you were silent and still.
You were made to carry a heavy cross, as you stumbled up the hill.

They nailed your precious hands that healed, and your precious feet;
But you are more than a conqueror and Satan you defeat.

Laid bare and naked for the entire world to see;
Your precious blood that was shed, gives us the Victory.

A spear was taken to pierce your side as you'd taken your last breath;
But you are Saviour, mighty God and conqueror over death.

They took you down and buried you in the garden tomb;
Your followers were very sad with heartbreak and gloom.

Don't you remember what he said, that he would rise again;
He took our sin and punishment, the Lamb of God was slain.

You took the keys off Satan, so that we could live;
For that I let you have my heart, of which I freely give.

On the third day you rose again so we could have salvation.
Jesus Christ, The Saviour, of every colour, creed and nation.

Thank you, Father, for sending Jesus, your one and only Son;
Thank you, Jesus, for your redeeming blood and all that you have done.

# Seasons and Events

# New Year

Another year is over and a new one will start;
What are you hoping for? What is in your heart?

Did you accomplish all you hoped for last year?
Or did you have regrets that filled you with fear?

The old year has gone, it is now the past;
Don't dwell on the bad things as they will not last.

Look to the present as it is a gift;
The present of Jesus, your soul he will lift.

Good things are coming and blessings your way;
Just hang on to Jesus because today is your day.

Rise up, my brothers and sisters too;
See what the Lord has in store for you.

He wants you, his children, to live a victorious life;
No more trouble, reproach or strife.

Children, rise up and go and possess the land;
Children, rise up declare Jesus and make your stand.

Your prayers are answered; it's all in God's hand;
You are his children; he knows what he's planned.

Be encouraged and be of good cheer;
It's time for your victory as this is your year.

# Spring

How I love the springtime, when darkness turns to light;
The beauty of the creation can be seen in its glory and might.

Spring is the start of new beginnings, of the earth being reborn;
Things that were dead now come alive in the breaking of the dawn.

The flowers start to break forth through the soil and spread their leaves;
Yet Solomon in all his splendour was not dressed like one of these.

The baby lambs can be found bleating in the fields.
The farmers sow their seed and expect an abundant yield.

The birds of the air break their shell as they come into the earth.
How I love the springtime as it speaks the earth's rebirth.

# Seasons

Seasons come and seasons go;
Sometimes sunshine, sometimes snow.

The winter chill and drawn dark nights;
December brings the Christmas lights.

Day by day, the days get lighter;
The hope of spring, the days get brighter.

New life is what we start seeing;
Things that are dormant come into being.

A splash of colour, of yellow and red;
Things come alive and no longer dead.

Baby lambs are seen in the field;
In the summer the farmer looks for his yield.

The warmth of sun fills the air; balmy nights do appear.

The sun goes down; slight winds unfold;
Colours change to reds and gold.

Leaves start to fall off the trees;
Gone is the cool summer breeze.

The dark winter nights start drawing in,
Again starts the cycle and where we begin.

# What Does Christmas Mean?

Christmas time, with busy streets of people rushing by;
Do they know its meaning or really care why?

The tills are busy ringing, money changing hands;
What does Christmas really mean, with all our frantic plans?

For some it's about presents, the fairy lights and food;
For some it's about family, friends and loved ones to include.

For some it's just a holiday to get some time off work;
Maybe a Christmas bonus would be an extra perk!

What does Christmas mean to you? Please give it your attention.
A gift was bought for you; which is priceless beyond all
comprehension.

# Birthday

God created you in his likeness; you are beautiful and wonderfully made.
May the light from your creator be full and never fade.

You were born for a purpose as we celebrate you today;
Let the favour of God be upon you, this is what I pray.

By God's grace he has added and given you another year;
May God keep you strong and steadfast and keep your heart from fear.

Let God's Love remain with you and rich blessings come your way;
Let the peace and joy of Jesus continue into your next birthday.

# Life

# Grace

God, give me the grace as I go about my day;
Help me to be a blessing to others, this is what I pray.

Help me not to get cross if someone pushes in front of me in a
queue; Let me think of Jesus and what would he do?

Help me not get wound up if my boss gets on my nerves;
Help me not to plot and think, he will get what he deserves.

When my dear beloved tells me, that I've done something wrong;
Oh Lord help me, to be still and to bite my tongue.

When other drivers make impolite gestures, that are obscene;
Help me not want to lay my hands on them, if you know what I
mean.

If someone is rude or hurtful, I will learn to smile;
In my head I'll count to ten to ensure I am not vile.

I know I am not perfect, help me to show love on my face.
Lord I just want to thank you, for your mercy and your grace.

# The I Poem

The world is all about I;
So I asked myself why?

i-Phone, i-Pad, i-Pod on;
I think my sense of self has gone.

Fast lane, working 9 to 5;
Trying hard to make a living, trying to survive.

I need the space to hear what you're saying in my ear;
To remove all the pressure, noise and fear.

Self-reflection, myself to exam;
Listen to the one who is called 'I Am'.

# Israel

I'd love to go to Israel, a place I've never seen;
I've love to go to Israel and walk where Jesus has been.

I'd like to go to Bethlehem, the place that you were born.
I'd like to visit the temple and see the curtain that was torn.

I'd love to touch the city walls, and sit within its gates,
See the Scribes and Pharisees, having their long debates.

I'd love to go to Canaan where you turned water into wine,
Yes, you are Lord Jesus Christ, the one true vine.

I'd love to see the places where you made the blind see,
You healed the sick and lonely and set the captives free.

I want to go to the garden where your sorrows were on your
heart;
You asked the Father to take your cup but you knew your part.

I want to go to Calvary where you shed your blood and died for
me.
It's where I cast my burdens and I know that I am free.

I want to see the empty tomb that confirms my salvation,
You are a God of Gentile and Jew, every creed, colour and Nation.

One day, with God's heavenly grace,
I'll see this wonderful country, God's beautiful place.

# Health

When I was young I took you for granted, you really meant nothing to me;
Now I am wiser, a little bit older, I need you in totality.

There is no amount of money that can buy you; there is no value or cost.
If I did not have you; I really would be lost.

It really is a blessing each day you stay with me;
There have been times, I cry: "Don't leave me hear my plea!"

I cannot count the days, weeks, months or years ahead;
The day will eventually come, when I finally rest my head.

One final word of wisdom that I'll impart to you;
You can starve for lots of money and amass a lot of wealth;
Nothing is as important, than having very good health.

# Keep Calm and Carry On

Keep calm and carry on;
I pray for a speedy recovery and all discomfort to be gone.

I pray that, through Christ, you can do all things;
I pray your strength to be renewed and you can mount on eagles'
wings.

Remember, you are unique, courageous and strong;
So just keep calm and keep going on.

# Israel part 2

I have been to Israel, its beauty I have seen;
I've been to the Mount of Olives, so lush and green.

I've been to Nazareth where Jesus was raised;
This is a place that was not highly praised.

I've been to the place of the Sermon on the Mount;
This is where Jesus taught us to give an account.
The sermon is also known as 'The Beatitudes';
This is where we learn to have the right attitudes.

I have touched and put a prayer inside the Wailing Wall;
I wore the white, blue and gold tallit prayer shawl.
I prayed for Jerusalem that she would find peace;
There would be love, unity and fighting would cease.

I've walked by the shore of Galilee; the water was so warm;
This is where Jesus silenced the storm.
I went into the River Jordan where Jesus was baptised.
This is where God said, "This is my beloved son" and the people
were surprised.

I've been to the small town of Bethlehem;
I've walked round the walls and cobbled streets of Jerusalem.
I've been to the Garden of Gethsemane;
Where Jesus shed his blood and tears for me.

I've been blessed to have walked and seen;
the places, where Jesus' feet have been.

I've entered into the Promised Land that God has given to you. If you've never been to Israel, I recommend that you do.

'Pray for the peace of Jerusalem: May those who love you be secure.'
Psalm 122:6 [NIV]

# Poems of Faith

# Holy Spirit

Holy Spirit, fill my soul;
Holy Spirit, make me whole.

Holy Spirit, do for me;
Holy Spirit set me free.

Holy Spirit give me joy;
Make my hands to your employ.

Holy Spirit, help me pray;
Help me find the words to say.

Jesus, Father, Son of God;
Help me learn and declare your word.

Spirit, help me overcome;
Thank you, Father, for your Son.

Spirit, lead me, take control;
Jesus, lover of my soul.

# Wind

I cannot see the wind, yet I feel its effects;
Like the invisible Holy Spirit that guides us and protects.

I have never seen the face of God or looked into his eyes;
Yet when I marvel at creation, there must be a God, that's no surprise.

The earth was made by the greatest designer the world has ever seen;
You won't find in Vogue, Prada or any other fashion magazine.

Everything is perfect, like how the planets orbit in space;
Yet people deny God because they haven't seen his face.

Have a little faith, my dear, be it small as a mustard seed;
Listen carefully, his voice you'll hear if you heed.

Look into the heavens and you will see sun, moon and star;
then shout: "Hallelujah! What a wonderful God you are!"

I cannot see the wind but yet I feel its power;
It reassures me that God is in every second, minute and hour.

# Mirror

When I look into the mirror, what do I see?
Is it the face of Jesus looking back at me?

They say I'm made in God's image, fearfully and wonderfully made;
And for this he loved me very much and a high price for me he
paid.

I am very precious in the Saviour's sight;
He bids his Angels charge over me to protect from any plight.

I am a wonderful human being;
The best creation has ever seen.

These words are not for me, they also apply to you;
As you are God's creation and very beautiful too.

# Your Face

I could not recognise your face;
Disfigured, looking out of place.

And yet I looked into your eyes;
Your love and compassion, there is no compromise.

The world in its sin had left you behind;
Caught in its trappings that easily blind.

Where can I find you? Where are you now?
I will walk with you, this is my vow.

You gave up everything for me;
You took my sin and punishment so I could be free.

The face that was disfigured; is now transfigured;
More radiant than the sun;
Thank you, Jesus, for being the lamb and all you have done.

# Seven

Seven is God's number of perfection, everything he has planned;
Do you know what he's done for you? Do you understand?

Seven times the blood was sprinkled, on the mercy seat;
Seven times Jesus shed his blood, for sin he did defeat.

The first drop was in the garden when he agonised for you;
The second time when they whipped him, so healing can come
through.

The third time was when the crown of thorns was put upon his
head;
The fourth and fifth times, when nails were put through each hand
that healed and also fed.

The sixth time when his feet where nailed, that walked this earth
from the start;
The seventh time was when his side was pierced and broken into
his heart.


S  is for Supernatural Speed; that God will meet our every need.
E  is for Everlasting Grace; so we are able to endure the trials we
face.
V  is for Victory, which God wants for you and me.
E  is for Elevation, that we promote the gospel to the people that
we see.
N  is for Nobility that we are joint heirs with him in heaven;
created in his perfection that is God's power of seven.

# Gift Poems

# Bag of Gold

I may not be able to give you a bag of gold;
Or give you riches that are untold.

But what I can give has been given to me;
It's a gift of words, that's what you will see.

A wise man said there's power in what we say;
I'm here to encourage and bring light to your way.

You have been faithful in the things of God;
The roads sometimes hard, where you have trod.

The crooked paths are being made straight;
God is always on time and never late.

He has seen your labour and your heart;
He is lifting you up and setting you apart.

He has seen your tears and your pain;
He says you are victorious and will not be put to shame.

God has good plans for you;
You will prosper in all that you do.

He will bless the work of your hands;
Your territory will spread to far-off lands.

Goodness and mercy will follow you;
It's in God's word, which is always true.

Glorious days are coming for you to behold;
You will see miracles outreaching and bold.

You will marvel at the things you've been told;
These words are your gift, God's bag of gold.

# The Blessing

A child of God like you is more valuable than a precious stone.
You are a comfort when I feel sad or alone.

You brighten my day with a laugh and smile;
I can count on you when I'm in the midst of a trial.

May God's blessing reign down on your life;
May you have favour instead of strife.

May you encounter God's angels today;
May they protect you and show you the way.

May you always have love in your heart;
May you always have compassion that will never depart.

May you have plenty and never know lack;
Anything that's been stolen you will get back.

Remember, you are a child of God, the apple of his eye;
God loves you very much and on him you can rely.

# Salvation Prayer

*Dear Father God, please come into my heart;*
*Please cleanse all my sins and give me a new start.*

*Thank you for sending Jesus to save me from my sins;*
*Thank you for the blood that heals me from within.*

*Thank you for your forgiveness, your grace and mercy too;*
*Today I give you my life and promise to follow you.*

*Thank you for my salvation and heaven is now my home;*
*You have promised to never leave me and I will never be alone.*

# About The Author

Hello, my name is Stevina Southwell and I live in Southampton, United Kingdom, where I was born and raised.

I have been writing poetry since the age of ten and like the rhythm and rhyme that poetry has to offer.

My inspirations are: Helen Steiner Rice, Maya Angelou, Pam Ayres and my grandfather, Harry Powell.

I enjoy writing poetry from a faith perspective, which aims to encourage and inspire the reader.

My desire is to see people reach their true potential, like the butterfly, which I have chosen as my cover.

The butterfly represents resurrection, which is core to the Christian Faith.

You may start out as a lowly caterpillar but then God in love takes you from caterpillar to chrysalis, then you break forth into a beautiful butterfly.

# Poetry Therapy

As a therapist I have found that poetry can be healing to both the writer and the reader.

In my own experiences I have found writing down thoughts and feelings cathartic when faced with challenging times which have been difficult to articulate.

The rhythm of poetry creates a sense of freedom where boundaries can be stretched and hidden meanings can be found in the narrative.

Similarly, in the Bible Jesus told stories in the form of parables, where there was always a hidden meaning or message, which I incorporate into my writing.

I hope these poems are a blessing which touches your life and you are able to break forth into the person God wants you to be.

Stevina x

Printed in Great Britain
by Amazon